Believe and Confess: Recovering the Biblical Gospel

Why Modern Evangelism Drifted—and How to Return to Biblical Clarity

Victor M. Font Jr.

A FontLife Publication, LLC

Believe and Confess: Recovering the Biblical Gospel

This book is presented for educational and informational purposes. Scripture quotations are taken from the King James Version (KJV), which is in the public domain.

All Scripture references, unless otherwise indicated, are from the King James Version.

Author: Victor M. Font Jr.

Publisher: A FontLife Publication, LLC.

Edition: First Edition

ISBN: 978-1-62422-065-4 (Print)

ISBN: 978-1-62422-066-1 (eBook)

Cover design and interior formatting by Victor M. Font Jr.

Images and illustrations in this publication were generated using DALL-E AI technology and are used under terms allowing commercial use. The author asserts ownership of the creative content and rights to commercially publish and distribute this work.

Printed in the United States of America

Dedication

To those who seek the truth of the Gospel—

Not in tradition,

Not in repetition,

Not in the comfort of familiar words—

But in the clarity of what God has spoken.

And to those who have asked, quietly and sincerely:

“Do I truly believe?”

May you find your answer not in a moment you remember,

but in the Savior who lives.

— Victor M. Font Jr.

Contents

Believe and Confess: Recovering the Biblical Gospel

There are phrases so familiar that they pass without question.

“Ask Jesus into your heart.”

“Pray this prayer.”

“Accept Christ.”

They are spoken in pulpits, printed in tracts, whispered in hospital rooms, and repeated in children’s ministries across generations. For many, they are tied to deeply personal moments—moments of conviction, relief, even joy.

And yet, a simple question presses in:

Where did this language come from?

More importantly—does it reflect how the Gospel is actually presented in Scripture?

The New Testament speaks with remarkable consistency about salvation. It does not present a formula to be recited, but a truth to be believed and a Lord to be confessed.

In Romans 10:9–10, the apostle Paul writes:

> "That if thou shalt confess with thy mouth the Lord Jesus, and shalt believe in thine heart that God hath raised him from the dead, thou shalt be saved.
>
> For with the heart man believeth unto righteousness; and with the mouth confession is made unto salvation."

The emphasis is unmistakable.

Not invitation—but belief.

Not a scripted prayer—but confession.

Not a moment manufactured—but faith rooted in the risen Christ.

Even in the most urgent and unlikely of circumstances, the pattern holds.

A dying man, condemned justly, turns his head toward another dying man—one he recognizes as King. There is no altar, no counselor, no prescribed words. Only a simple appeal:

"Lord, remember me when thou comest into thy kingdom."

And the response comes with equal clarity:

"Today shalt thou be with me in paradise."

No formula. No ritual. No intermediary language.

Just faith.

This book is not written to dismiss the sincerity of those who have used familiar phrases, nor to question the reality of genuine conversion that may have occurred alongside them. God is not constrained by our vocabulary, and He has drawn many to Himself despite our imprecision.

But sincerity does not sanctify language.

And when language begins to drift, understanding is never far behind.

Over time, the way the Gospel is presented has shifted—subtly at first, then systematically. What was once proclaimed as a call to believe and confess has, in many contexts, been reduced to an invitation to perform an action. The center of gravity has moved from Christ Himself to the individual's response to Him.

This is not a small shift.

Because the question of salvation is not ultimately:

"Did I say the right words?"

It is:

"Do I believe on the Lord Jesus Christ?"

And if that distinction is blurred, even unintentionally, the consequences are not merely theological—they are deeply personal. Assurance becomes anchored to a past moment rather than a present reality. Faith risks being replaced by memory. Confidence may rest not in Christ, but in an experience.

This book is an attempt to recover clarity.

Not by innovation, but by returning to what has already been said.

Not by introducing something new, but by removing what has been added.

Not by complicating the Gospel, but by letting it speak for itself.

We will examine how salvation is presented in Scripture, how the language surrounding it developed over time, and how well-intended simplifications may have introduced unintended confusion. We will consider the difference between metaphor and mechanism, between illustration and instruction, between what is helpful and what is essential.

The goal is not to win an argument.

The goal is to remove obstacles.

So that what remains is simple, direct, and unmistakable:

Believe on the Lord Jesus Christ.

Confess Him as Lord.

And rest, not in the words you have spoken, but in the One who has been raised from the dead.

Chapter 1

The Language of Salvation in Scripture

If we are to recover clarity, we must begin with a simple discipline:

Let Scripture define its own terms.

Not our traditions.

Not our methods.

Not our preferred phrasing.

Because when it comes to salvation, precision is not optional. The stakes are too high to rely on assumption or familiarity. The question is not how we have learned to speak about salvation, but how the Word of God actually presents it.

And when we look carefully, a pattern emerges—consistent, direct, and strikingly free of the language that has become so common today.

The Central Question

Across the New Testament, the issue is never framed as:

“Will you invite Jesus into your heart?”

Instead, it is consistently framed as:

- Who is Jesus?
- Do you believe Him?
- Will you confess Him as Lord?

Salvation is not presented as a procedure to complete, but as a reality to embrace—a response to truth, not a script to recite.

The Testimony of the Gospels

The preaching of Jesus Himself sets the foundation.

In Gospel of Mark 1:15, His message is summarized with unmistakable clarity:

“The time is fulfilled, and the kingdom of God is at hand: repent ye, and believe the gospel.”

Two imperatives:

- Repent
- Believe

There is no accompanying instruction to perform a verbal formula. No indication that salvation hinges on repeating specific words. The call is directed to the heart and mind—to a turning and a trusting.

This pattern continues throughout the Gospels.

In the Gospel of John, belief is central and repeated:

> "That whosoever believeth in him should not perish, but have eternal life." (John 3:16)

> "He that believeth on the Son hath everlasting life." (John 3:36)

John's Gospel, written explicitly so that readers might believe (John 20:31), never instructs the reader to "invite Jesus into your heart." Instead, it calls for faith in the person of Christ—His identity, His authority, and His work.

Belief is not presented as a vague feeling, nor as mere intellectual agreement. It is trust—resting in who Christ is and what He has accomplished.

The Witness of Acts

If the Gospels establish the message, the Acts of the Apostles shows how that message was proclaimed.

Here, we are not dealing with theory, but with practice.

On the day of Pentecost, Peter preaches Christ crucified and risen. The crowd, convicted, asks a direct question:

"What shall we do?"

Peter's response (Acts 2:38):

"Repent, and be baptized every one of you in the name of Jesus Christ for the remission of sins..."

Again, the emphasis is not on reciting a prayer, but on repentance and identification with Christ.

Later, in Acts 16:30–31, a jailer asks:

"Sirs, what must I do to be saved?"

The answer is immediate and unambiguous:

"Believe on the Lord Jesus Christ, and thou shalt be saved..."

Not "repeat after me."

Not "invite Him in."

Believe.

That is the consistent apostolic answer.

The Clarity of Paul's Theology

Nowhere is the language of salvation more distilled than in Romans 10:9–10:

> "That if thou shalt confess with thy mouth the Lord Jesus, and shalt believe in thine heart that God hath raised him from the dead, thou shalt be saved."

Here, two elements are inseparably joined:

- **Belief in the heart** — that God has raised Jesus from the dead
- **Confession with the mouth** — that Jesus is Lord

This is not a formula. It is a description.

Paul is not prescribing a scripted sequence of words, but describing the natural expression of genuine faith. The mouth confesses what the heart believes.

The order matters.

Belief produces confession—not the other way around.

And the object of that belief is specific:

- The risen Christ
- His lordship
- His victory over death

This is not generic spirituality. It is anchored in historical, theological reality.

A Case Study: The Thief on the Cross

Few examples are more instructive than the account found in the Gospel of Luke 23:39–43.

A man, facing imminent death, turns to Jesus and says:

> "Lord, remember me when thou comest into thy kingdom."

In that brief statement, several truths are evident:

- He acknowledges his own guilt
- He recognizes Jesus' innocence
- He affirms Jesus' kingship and coming kingdom
- He appeals to Him in faith

There is no formal structure. No guided prayer. No theological vocabulary beyond what the moment demands.

And yet, the response from Christ is immediate:

> "Today shalt thou be with me in paradise."

If ever there were a moment to require precision of wording, this would be it.

And yet, none is required.

Because salvation does not rest on phrasing—it rests on faith.

What Is Not There

At this point, the absence becomes as important as the presence.

Across the Gospels, Acts, and the Epistles, we do not find:

- Instructions to "ask Jesus into your heart"
- A prescribed "sinner's prayer"
- A required verbal formula for salvation

This is not an argument from silence alone. It is an argument from contrast.

Scripture is not silent about salvation. It speaks often, clearly, and consistently.

And in all that clarity, it never once presents salvation as the result of inviting Christ into one's heart through a specific prayer.

Why This Matters

At first glance, the difference may seem small—perhaps even semantic.

After all, one might argue, does not "asking Jesus into your heart" simply express belief?

At times, perhaps it does.

But language shapes understanding.

And when the language of Scripture is replaced, even with good intentions, the risk is not merely stylistic—it is conceptual.

A shift begins to occur:

- From **believing in Christ** to **performing an action toward Christ**
- From **trusting His finished work** to **relying on a personal moment**
- From **ongoing faith** to **past experience**

Over time, the emphasis can subtly move away from Christ Himself and toward the individual's response to Him.

And when that happens, assurance may no longer rest in the object of faith, but in the memory of an event.

Returning to Simplicity

The New Testament does not complicate salvation.

It does not require theological sophistication, emotional intensity, or verbal precision.

It requires faith.

- Faith in who Jesus is
- Faith in what He has done
- Faith expressed openly, without shame

To believe.

To confess.

That is the language of Scripture.

And if we are to speak with clarity, it must become our language again.

Chapter 2

The Preaching of the Apostles

If the Gospels establish the message, then Acts of the Apostles reveals how that message was proclaimed.

Here we move from instruction to execution. From what Jesus taught to how His apostles preached. From foundation to function.

And what we find is not a variety of methods, but a remarkable consistency of message.

A Gospel Proclaimed, Not Negotiated

One of the first things that becomes clear in Acts is that the apostles did not present the Gospel as an invitation to consider, but as a declaration to confront.

They proclaimed:

- Jesus was crucified

- Jesus was raised
- Jesus is Lord

And they called for a response.

Not a scripted response. Not a guided prayer. But a response rooted in conviction.

Pentecost: Conviction Before Instruction

In Acts 2, Peter stands before a crowd in Jerusalem and delivers what is, in many ways, the first public proclamation of the risen Christ.

He does not begin with an appeal.

He begins with a declaration:

- Jesus of Nazareth was attested by God
- He was crucified by lawless hands
- God raised Him from the dead
- He is now exalted as Lord and Christ

The result is immediate and profound:

> "Now when they heard this, they were pricked in their heart..."

Conviction precedes instruction.

Only after the crowd is cut to the heart do they ask:

> "What shall we do?"

Peter's response (Acts 2:38) is direct:

> "Repent, and be baptized every one of you in the name of Jesus Christ for the remission of sins..."

Notice what is absent.

There is no moment where Peter leads the crowd in a prayer. No formula to repeat. No phrase to memorize.

Instead:

- Repentance
- Identification with Christ
- The promise of forgiveness

The response is not manufactured—it is the natural outcome of conviction.

The Pattern Repeats

As Acts unfolds, this pattern is not abandoned. It is reinforced.

Acts 3 — Peter in the Temple

Peter again proclaims Christ—His death, His resurrection, His fulfillment of prophecy.

His call is simple:

> "Repent ye therefore, and be converted, that your sins may be blotted out..." (Acts 3:19)

No formula. No ritualized language.

Repent. Turn. Be restored.

Acts 5 — Apostolic Summary

The apostles summarize their own message:

> "Him hath God exalted... to be a Prince and a Saviour, for to give repentance to Israel, and forgiveness of sins." (Acts 5:31)

Again, repentance and forgiveness—not procedural steps, but relational realities grounded in Christ.

The Gentile Inclusion: Same Message, Same Response

When the Gospel moves beyond Israel, the message does not change.

In Acts 10, Peter is sent to the house of Cornelius, a Gentile.

As Peter speaks of Jesus—His life, death, and resurrection—the response occurs even before a formal conclusion:

> "...whosoever believeth in him shall receive remission of sins." (Acts 10:43)

And as he speaks, the Holy Spirit falls on those who hear.

No prayer is led. No invitation is extended in the modern sense.

They hear. They believe. God acts.

The simplicity is almost uncomfortable for those accustomed to structured responses.

The Philippian Jailer: The Question Answered

Perhaps the most direct question in all of Acts is found in Acts 16.

A jailer, shaken and desperate, asks:

> "Sirs, what must I do to be saved?"

If ever there were a moment to provide a precise formula, this would be it.

The answer given is striking in its brevity:

> "Believe on the Lord Jesus Christ, and thou shalt be saved..." (Acts 16:31)

That is the answer.

Not expanded. Not qualified with a script. Not followed by instructions to repeat specific words.

Believe.

The apostles do not seem concerned that the answer is too simple. They do not attempt to safeguard it with additional language.

They trust the clarity of the Gospel itself.

Public Confession: Faith That Speaks

While there is no prescribed prayer, there is a consistent expectation:

Faith is not hidden.

In Acts, belief is often accompanied by:

- Baptism
- Public identification
- Open confession

This aligns directly with Romans 10:10:

> "...with the mouth confession is made unto salvation."

Confession is not a ritual—it is the outward expression of inward belief.

It is not the means of salvation, but its evidence.

What the Apostles Did Not Do

At this point, the pattern is difficult to ignore.

The apostles did not:

- Lead crowds in a standardized prayer
- Instruct individuals to “ask Jesus into their heart”
- Emphasize a moment of verbal repetition as the point of salvation

This is not due to oversight.

These were men entrusted with the Gospel itself. If such a practice were essential, it would not be absent—it would be central.

Instead, what we see is confidence in the message:

- Proclaim Christ
- Call for repentance
- Call for belief
- Trust God to work

The Role of Urgency Without Manipulation

Acts is filled with urgency.

People respond immediately:

- Three thousand at Pentecost
- The Ethiopian eunuch on the road
- The jailer in the night

But urgency is not manufactured.

There is no emotional escalation, no prolonged atmosphere-building, no repetition designed to produce a response.

The urgency comes from truth itself:

- The reality of sin
- The certainty of judgment
- The proclamation of a risen Lord

The response is serious because the message is serious.

A Subtle but Critical Distinction

It would be easy to assume that modern methods are simply expansions of apostolic practice.

But there is a subtle shift:

- In Acts, the message creates the response
- In many modern contexts, the method attempts to produce the response

That distinction is not merely methodological—it is theological.

Because it raises an important question:

Is salvation the result of hearing and believing the Gospel...

or the result of completing a guided response?

The apostles seem to have no confusion.

They preach Christ—and call men to believe.

Returning to Apostolic Clarity

The preaching in Acts is not complex, but it is precise.

It is centered on:

- The person of Jesus Christ
- The reality of His resurrection
- The necessity of repentance
- The call to believe

And it trusts that this is enough.

No embellishment.

No replacement language.

No reliance on formula.

Just the Gospel—proclaimed with clarity, and received by faith.

If we are to recover the biblical Gospel, we must not only examine what was said, but how it was said.

And in Acts, the pattern is unmistakable:

Preach Christ.

Call for belief.

Trust God with the result.

Chapter 3

Belief and Confession in the Epistle to the Romans

If the preaching in Acts shows us how the Gospel was proclaimed, then Romans shows us how it is understood.

Here, the apostle Paul is not addressing a crowd in the moment of conviction. He is writing with precision—laying out the theological foundation beneath the message the apostles preached.

And in Romans 10, he brings the language of salvation into sharp focus.

The Righteousness That Comes by Faith

Paul begins by contrasting two kinds of righteousness:

- A righteousness based on the law
- A righteousness based on faith

The distinction is not minor—it is absolute.

The law demands performance.

Faith rests in provision.

Paul is not offering a hybrid. He is making a clean break.

Salvation is not achieved. It is received.

And that reception is defined not by action, but by belief.

The Word Is Near

In Romans 10:6–8, Paul makes a remarkable statement:

> "The word is nigh thee, even in thy mouth, and in thy heart..."

Salvation is not distant, hidden, or inaccessible. It does not require extraordinary effort or spiritual ascent.

It is near.

Not because it is easy—but because it has been revealed.

And that revelation centers on Christ.

The Core Declaration

Paul then articulates what is perhaps the clearest summary of salvation in all of Scripture:

> "That if thou shalt confess with thy mouth the Lord Jesus, and shalt believe in thine heart that God hath

> raised him from the dead, thou shalt be saved." (Romans 10:9)

Two elements—distinct, but inseparable:

- **Belief in the heart**
- **Confession with the mouth**

This is not a formula to perform. It is a reality to describe.

Paul is not prescribing a sequence of words. He is describing the nature of saving faith.

Belief in the Heart

First, belief.

Not superficial agreement. Not cultural familiarity. Not intellectual curiosity.

Belief "in the heart" speaks to:

- Conviction
- Trust
- Reliance

And the content of that belief is specific:

> "...that God hath raised him from the dead..."

This is not incidental.

The resurrection is the validation of everything Christ claimed:

- His identity as Son of God
- His authority as Lord
- His victory over sin and death

To believe in the resurrection is to affirm that Christ's work is complete and sufficient.

It is to rest in what God has done—not in what we might do.

Confession with the Mouth

Second, confession.

> "...confess with thy mouth the Lord Jesus..."

This is not merely speaking His name.

It is declaring His lordship.

To confess "Jesus is Lord" in the first-century context was not a casual statement. It was a declaration of allegiance:

- Above Caesar
- Above culture
- Above self

It was public. It was costly. It was definitive.

Confession, then, is not a ritualized statement—it is the outward expression of inward belief.

The mouth speaks because the heart believes.

The Order Matters

Paul reinforces this in Romans 10:10:

> "For with the heart man believeth unto righteousness; and with the mouth confession is made unto salvation."

Notice the flow:

- Belief → righteousness
- Confession → expression of that reality

Confession does not create salvation. It reveals it.

This is a critical distinction.

Because when confession is misunderstood as a mechanism—something that produces salvation—it risks replacing faith with performance.

And that is precisely what Paul is arguing against.

No Distinction, No Barrier

Paul continues:

> "For the scripture saith, Whosoever believeth on him shall not be ashamed." (Romans 10:11)

And again:

> "For there is no difference... for the same Lord over all is rich unto all that call upon him." (Romans 10:12)

Salvation is universal in scope—not in outcome, but in availability.

There is no category of person for whom this does not apply.

And the condition remains unchanged:

Belief.

Not background.

Not knowledge level.

Not eloquence.

Belief.

Calling on the Name of the Lord

Paul then writes:

> "For whosoever shall call upon the name of the Lord shall be saved." (Romans 10:13)

This verse is often cited to support the idea of a prayer-based formula.

But Paul is not introducing a new method. He is reinforcing the same reality.

To “call upon the name of the Lord” is not to recite a phrase.

It is to appeal to Him in faith.

It is what the thief on the cross did.

It is what the tax collector did.

It is what countless others did—without script, without structure, but with sincerity rooted in belief.

Calling is the expression of faith—not its substitute.

The Context of Hearing

Paul immediately anchors this in the broader process:

> “How then shall they call on him in whom they have not believed?
>
> and how shall they believe in him of whom they have not heard?” (Romans 10:14)

The sequence is clear:

- The Gospel is preached
- It is heard
- It is believed
- The believer calls upon the Lord

The foundation is always the same:

> Faith comes by hearing, and hearing by the word of God (Romans 10:17).

Not by repetition.

Not by coaching.

Not by formula.

By hearing—and believing.

What Paul Does Not Say

Given the precision of this passage, the absence is again instructive.

Paul does not say:

- "Repeat this prayer and you will be saved"
- "Invite Jesus into your heart"
- "Say these words after me"

He does not reduce salvation to a moment of verbal expression.

Instead, he anchors it in:

- The content of the Gospel
- The reality of belief
- The inevitability of confession

The Risk of Reversal

When modern language shifts the emphasis, a subtle reversal can occur:

- Confession becomes the means, rather than the expression
- The prayer becomes the focus, rather than Christ
- Assurance rests in what was said, rather than what is believed

This is not merely a difference in phrasing.

It is a difference in foundation.

Because if salvation is tied—even unintentionally—to the act of speaking certain words, then the question of assurance becomes:

"Did I say it correctly?"

Rather than:

"Do I believe on the Lord Jesus Christ?"

Paul leaves no room for that confusion.

The Simplicity That Remains

At its core, Romans 10 is not complex.

It is direct. It is clear. It is sufficient.

- Believe in your heart

- Confess with your mouth

Not as a formula—but as a reality.

Not as a method—but as a response.

Not as something you perform—but as something that flows from faith.

This is the language of salvation.

And if we are to recover the biblical Gospel, we must resist the urge to improve upon it.

Because nothing we add will make it clearer.

And much that we add may, in time, obscure it.

Chapter 4

The Thief on the Cross: A Case Study in Saving Faith

There are moments in Scripture where theology is not merely taught—it is displayed.

The account of the thief on the cross is one of those moments.

Stripped of ceremony, removed from structure, and pressed under the weight of immediate death, this scene presents salvation in its most unembellished form. There is no time for process. No opportunity for ritual. No environment for guided response.

And yet, what occurs in this moment has served for centuries as one of the clearest illustrations of saving faith.

If we are to understand what is essential—and what is not—this is where we must look.

The Setting: Judgment and Finality

The account in Luke 23:39–43 places us at the crucifixion.

Three men hang on crosses:

- One is innocent
- Two are guilty

Both criminals begin in similar positions—condemned, suffering, and facing death.

But what unfolds reveals a profound divergence.

One joins in the mockery:

> "If thou be Christ, save thyself and us."

The other responds with rebuke:

> "Dost not thou fear God, seeing thou art in the same condemnation?"

In that moment, something has already changed.

Recognition of Guilt

The second thief continues:

> "And we indeed justly; for we receive the due reward of our deeds..."

This is the first mark of genuine repentance:

- No deflection
- No excuse
- No comparison

He does not minimize his condition. He acknowledges it fully.

This aligns with the broader testimony of Scripture:

Repentance begins where self-justification ends.

There is no salvation apart from this recognition.

Recognition of Christ

He then says:

> "...but this man hath done nothing amiss."

In the midst of agony, he discerns what others have rejected:

- Jesus is innocent
- Jesus is different
- Jesus does not belong under this judgment

But he goes further.

Turning to Jesus, he says:

"Lord, remember me when thou comest into thy kingdom."

This statement is astonishing in its depth.

Consider what it contains:

- **Acknowledgment of lordship** — "Lord"
- **Belief in a coming kingdom** — beyond the cross
- **Confidence in Christ's authority** — to remember, to receive

There is no visible kingdom. No display of power. No immediate evidence.

Only a dying man—and yet, he believes.

This is faith.

Not informed by circumstance, but grounded in recognition.

No Formula, Only Faith

At this point, the absence of structure becomes impossible to ignore.

There is:

- No sinner's prayer
- No instruction to repeat specific words
- No guided process

No one leads him. No one coaches him. No one clarifies his phrasing.

And yet, everything necessary is present:

- Repentance
- Belief
- Confession

Not as separate steps—but as a unified response.

He does not perform salvation.

He expresses faith.

The Response of Christ

Jesus replies:

> "Verily I say unto thee, Today shalt thou be with me in paradise."

The immediacy is striking.

- No delay
- No condition added
- correction of wording

Christ does not say:

"You should have said more."

"You need to repeat that differently."

"You must complete this process."

He affirms the reality of what has already occurred.

Faith has been expressed. Salvation is granted.

What This Case Reveals

This moment serves as a theological anchor.

It demonstrates, with clarity that cannot be softened:

Salvation does not depend on:

- Location (there is no church)
- Ritual (there is no baptism)
- Language (there is no prescribed formula)
- Timing (it occurs in the final hours of life)

It depends on faith.

Faith that recognizes:

- Personal guilt
- Christ's identity
- Christ's authority
- Christ's sufficiency

And responds accordingly.

A Challenge to Modern Assumptions

If we are honest, this account confronts several modern assumptions.

It raises uncomfortable questions:

If a specific prayer were essential, why is it absent here?

If precise wording were required, why is none given?

If salvation depended on a guided response, why is none provided?

This is not an argument built on exception—it is a demonstration of essence.

In the most constrained circumstances imaginable, what remains is what is necessary.

And what remains is faith.

Not an Argument Against Expression

It must be said clearly:

The thief does speak.

He does call out to Christ.

He does express his belief verbally.

But his words are not a formula—they are a reflection.

They are not prescribed—they are personal.

This is an important distinction.

The issue is not whether someone speaks.

The issue is whether salvation is tied to *what* is spoken—or to *what is believed.*

In this case, the words matter only because they reveal the heart.

The Simplicity We Resist

There is something in us that resists this simplicity.

We prefer structure.

We prefer clarity in steps.

We prefer something we can point to and say, "That is when it happened."

But Scripture repeatedly brings us back to something less tangible—and more profound:

Faith.

Not manufactured.

Not scripted.

Not controlled.

Real.

The End That Clarifies the Beginning

It is fitting that this account occurs at the end of Christ's earthly life.

Because in that final moment, the Gospel is not explained—it is embodied.

A sinner, acknowledging his guilt, turns to Christ in faith.

And Christ receives him.

No additions.

No qualifications.

No requirements beyond what has already been met in Him.

This is the Gospel in its purest form.

And it leaves us with a question that echoes beyond the cross:

Not, "Have you said the right words?"

But, "Do you see Him—and do you believe?"

Chapter 5

Repentance: Turning to God

There are few words in Scripture more essential—and more misunderstood—than the word *repent*.

Jesus said, "Repent and believe the Gospel."

The apostles preached, "Repent."

And yet today, many hear that word and are unsure what it means.

Some hear it and think of anger.

Others think of guilt.

Some avoid it altogether.

But if we misunderstand repentance, we misunderstand the Gospel itself.

So we begin with a simple question:

What does it mean to repent?

A Word That Means "Turn"

At its most basic level, repentance means this:

To turn.

If a person is walking down a road that leads in the wrong direction, repentance is what happens when they stop, turn around, and begin walking the other way.

That is the picture.

You were going one way.

Now you are going another.

It is not complicated—but it is decisive.

It Begins in the Heart

Repentance is not first about what you do.

It is about how you think.

It is a change in how you see:

- Yourself
- Your sin
- God

Before repentance, a person may think:

"I am not that bad."

"My choices are my own."

"God is distant or irrelevant."

After repentance begins, something shifts:

"I have sinned."

"I am accountable."

"God is holy—and I must answer to Him."

This change does not come from effort.

It comes from truth being seen clearly.

More Than Feeling Sorry

Repentance often includes sorrow.

A person may feel conviction, regret, or grief over sin.

But repentance is not the same as feeling bad.

It is possible to feel sorry and never change direction.

Repentance says:

"I was wrong—and I am turning."

It is not just emotion.

It is movement.

Turning Away—and Turning Toward

Repentance is often described as turning away from sin.

That is true—but it is only half the picture.

Repentance is also turning **toward God**.

These two movements happen together:

- Away from sin
- Toward God

If a person tries only to stop doing wrong, they have not fully repented.

Because repentance is not simply behavior management.

It is a reorientation of the heart.

A Child Can Understand It

If we were to explain repentance to a child, we might say:

"I was going my way.

Now I turn and go God's way."

Or even more simply:

"I was wrong—and I am turning to God."

That is repentance.

Simple enough for a child to understand.

Serious enough to change a life.

Repentance and Faith Belong Together

In Scripture, repentance and belief are never separated.

They are not two different responses.

They are two sides of the same turning.

When a person repents:

- They turn away from sin
- They turn toward Christ

When a person believes:

- They trust Christ
- They rely on Him

These are not competing ideas—they are connected.

You cannot truly turn to Christ without turning from what separates you from Him.

And you cannot truly turn from sin without turning to Christ.

What Repentance Is Not

Because the word has been misunderstood, it is important to be clear.

Repentance is not:

- Saying certain words
- Repeating a prayer
- Making a promise to do better
- Trying harder to fix yourself

It is not a performance.

It is not something you complete.

It is something that happens when truth changes you.

What Repentance Produces

When repentance is real, it produces change.

Not perfection.

Not instant transformation in every area.

But a real shift.

The direction of a person's life changes.

What they once loved, they begin to question.

What they once ignored, they begin to pursue.

There is a new orientation.

Not because they are forcing it—but because something inside has changed.

Why This Matters

If repentance is reduced to feeling sorry, people may believe they have repented when they have not.

If repentance is replaced with a formula, people may believe they are saved because they spoke words.

But Scripture never presents repentance that way.

It presents it as a turning:

- From sin
- To God

And that turning is inseparable from faith.

Returning to the Words of Christ

When Jesus said, "Repent and believe the Gospel," He was not giving two unrelated commands.

He was calling for a complete response.

Turn.

Believe.

Not outwardly only—but inwardly, truly, and completely.

And where that happens, everything begins to change.

Chapter 6

Baptism: Identification, Not Salvation

Few subjects generate more confusion in discussions about salvation than baptism.

For some, it is seen as essential—something that must occur for salvation to be complete.

For others, it is minimized or treated as optional to the point of irrelevance.

Scripture allows for neither extreme.

To understand baptism correctly, we must place it where the New Testament places it:

Not as the means of salvation—

but as the response to it.

What Baptism Is Not

The New Testament never presents baptism as the thing that causes a person to be saved.

Salvation is consistently tied to:

- Belief
- Repentance
- Faith in Christ

As we have already seen in Romans 10, salvation is grounded in belief in the heart and confession of Christ as Lord.

The thief on the cross, hanging beside Christ, was never baptized.

And yet Christ said:

> "Today shalt thou be with me in paradise."

If baptism were required for salvation, this moment would be impossible to explain.

It is not.

Because salvation does not depend on water.

It depends on Christ.

Then Why Baptism?

If baptism does not save, why is it so consistently present in the New Testament?

Because it is the God-ordained way a believer publicly identifies with Christ.

Baptism is not about becoming something.

It is about declaring what has already happened.

A Picture of Death and Life

Paul explains this clearly in Romans 6:3–4:

> "Know ye not, that so many of us as were baptized into Jesus Christ were baptized into his death?
>
> Therefore we are buried with him by baptism into death: that like as Christ was raised up from the dead... even so we also should walk in newness of life."

Baptism is a picture.

- Going under the water — death and burial
- Coming out of the water — resurrection and new life

It is not the event that causes these realities.

It is the symbol that proclaims them.

The Ethiopian Eunuch: Order Matters

One of the clearest examples of baptism in context is found in Acts 8:26–38.

Philip encounters an Ethiopian eunuch reading Isaiah. He explains the Gospel—specifically, the identity and work of Jesus Christ.

After hearing the message, the eunuch responds:

> "See, here is water; what doth hinder me to be baptized?"

This is an important moment.

He does not ask how to be saved.

He has already heard—and believed—the message Philip preached.

Philip's response clarifies the order:

> "If thou believest with all thine heart, thou mayest."

Belief comes first.

Baptism follows.

This is not incidental.

It is intentional.

The eunuch then declares:

> "I believe that Jesus Christ is the Son of God."

Only after this confession does baptism occur.

The sequence is unmistakable:

- The Gospel is preached
- Faith is present
- Confession is made
- Baptism follows

Not as a requirement for salvation—but as a response to it.

Baptism by Immersion

The same passage also provides insight into the mode of baptism.

The text tells us:

> "...they went down both into the water... and he baptized him.
>
> And when they were come up out of the water..."

This language is not accidental.

It reflects immersion:

- Going down into the water
- Coming up out of the water

This aligns with the imagery described in Romans 6:

- Burial (going under)
- Resurrection (coming up)

Sprinkling does not reflect burial.

Pouring does not reflect rising.

Immersion alone preserves the full picture that baptism is intended to convey.

Identification with Christ

In baptism, a believer is saying:

"I belong to Him."

"I identify with His death."

"I identify with His resurrection."

It is a public act of allegiance.

Not unlike confession with the mouth—it makes visible what has already occurred in the heart.

The Consistent Pattern

In Acts of the Apostles, we see a repeated pattern:

- The Gospel is preached
- People believe
- They are baptized

The order matters.

Belief comes first.

Baptism follows.

Not as a condition—but as a response.

It is immediate, often without delay, not because it completes salvation—but because it declares it.

The Danger of Misplacing It

When baptism is placed before faith—or treated as the cause of salvation—confusion follows.

It shifts the focus from:

- What Christ has done

to

- What we must do

It turns a declaration into a requirement.

And once that shift occurs, assurance can begin to rest in an action rather than in Christ Himself.

A Necessary Clarification

It is sometimes said, in an effort to correct misunderstanding, that baptism is "just getting wet."

There is a sense in which this is true.

The water itself has no power to save.

It does not cleanse sin.

It does not regenerate the heart.

But to stop there would be to miss something important.

Because while baptism does not save—it is not meaningless.

It is:

- An act of obedience
- A public identification
- A visible proclamation of invisible faith

The water does not save.

But what it represents matters deeply.

Why It Still Matters

If baptism does not save, some may ask:

“Then why should it matter?”

Because Christ commanded it.

Because the apostles practiced it.

Because it is the first outward step of obedience for a believer.

Not to become saved—but because they are.

To refuse it is not to lose salvation—but it does raise a different question:

If one truly believes, why resist identifying with Him?

Holding the Balance

Scripture holds baptism in a clear and balanced place:

- Not as the means of salvation
- Not as an optional afterthought

But as the natural, immediate expression of faith.

It follows belief.

It does not produce it.

Returning to Clarity

In the same way that salvation is not found in repeating certain words, it is not found in performing certain actions.

Not in a prayer.

Not in water.

But in Christ.

Believed in the heart.

Confessed with the mouth.

And then—lived out, openly, without shame.

Chapter 7

From Early Church to Reformation: A Gospel Without Formulas

Before examining how modern language developed, it is worth asking a simple question:

How did the church speak about salvation for most of its history?

If phrases like "ask Jesus into your heart" or the use of a standardized "sinner's prayer" are essential to the Gospel, we would expect to find them early—clearly present, widely practiced, and consistently taught.

But when we look at the historical record, we find something very different.

For centuries, the church proclaimed salvation without formulas.

The Early Church: Confession and Baptism

In the generations immediately following the apostles, the message of salvation remained closely aligned with the pattern found in Scripture.

The focus was on:

- Repentance
- Faith in Christ
- Public confession
- Baptism

Those coming to faith were instructed, often over time, in what they believed. When they were baptized, they would confess that Jesus is Lord.

This was not a scripted prayer for salvation.

It was a declaration of allegiance.

Salvation was not tied to repeating specific words, but to believing in Christ and identifying with Him openly.

Clarity Without Simplification

The early church did not appear concerned that the Gospel was too complex.

There is no evidence of attempts to reduce it to a repeatable formula for the sake of accessibility.

Instead, there was a confidence that:

- The message of Christ was sufficient
- The Spirit of God was active
- Faith would be expressed, not manufactured

This did not mean the process was always immediate.

In many cases, instruction preceded baptism.
Understanding was cultivated. Commitment was examined.

Not to complicate salvation—but to take it seriously.

The Medieval Period: Structure Without Formula

As the church moved into the medieval period, the structure around salvation became more formalized.

Sacraments were emphasized. Systems developed. The church became an institution with defined processes.

But even here, we still do not find:

- A "sinner's prayer" as a required step
- Language about "inviting Jesus into your heart"
- A moment defined by repeating a specific phrase

Whatever theological complications emerged during this period, salvation was not reduced to a verbal formula.

The emphasis remained on participation, confession, and the life of the church—however imperfectly understood.

The Reformation: Faith Recovered

The Protestant Reformation marked a decisive return to the authority of Scripture.

Figures such as Martin Luther and John Calvin challenged the structures that had obscured the Gospel and reasserted a foundational truth:

Justification is by faith alone.

This was not a new idea.

It was a recovery.

The Reformers pointed back to passages like Romans 10, insisting that salvation rests not on works, not on ritual, and not on human effort—but on faith in Christ.

And yet, even in this renewed clarity, we still do not find the language that has become so common today.

The Reformers did not instruct people to:

- "Ask Jesus into your heart"
- Repeat a specific prayer
- Anchor their assurance in a past verbal moment

Instead, they called people to:

- Trust in Christ
- Rest in His finished work
- Believe the promises of God

Confession Without Formula

Confessions of faith were written during this time—carefully structured summaries of doctrine.

But these were not tools for conversion.

They were tools for clarity.

They helped articulate what was believed—not prescribe what must be said in order to be saved.

This distinction matters.

Because it reinforces a consistent pattern across centuries:

The church has always emphasized belief and confession.

But it has not historically reduced those realities to a required script.

What Is Missing—and Why It Matters

At this point, the absence becomes difficult to ignore.

Across:

- The early church
- The medieval period
- The Reformation

We do not find the now-familiar language of:

- "Inviting Jesus into your heart"
- A standardized "sinner's prayer"

- A defined moment of salvation tied to repeating specific words

This does not prove that such language is inherently wrong.

But it does raise an important question:

If this were essential to the Gospel, why is it absent for so much of church history?

The answer is not that earlier generations were unaware.

It is that they were working from a different framework.

One in which:

- Faith was central
- Confession was natural
- Salvation was understood as a work of God—not a response to a scripted invitation

The Weight of Continuity

There is a certain weight that comes with historical continuity.

When a pattern remains consistent across centuries, it deserves attention.

And when a new pattern emerges later—especially one that shifts emphasis—it deserves examination.

The issue is not tradition for its own sake.

The issue is alignment.

Does our language reflect the same clarity found in Scripture—and echoed through the church's history?

Or has something been added that, over time, has begun to reshape understanding?

Preparing for the Shift

By the end of the Reformation, the Gospel had been clearly articulated:

- Salvation by grace
- Through faith
- In Christ alone

No formulas.

No required phrases.

No scripted entry point.

And yet, in the centuries that follow, something begins to change.

Not immediately. Not all at once.

But gradually, the emphasis begins to shift:

From proclamation...

to persuasion.

From belief...

to decision.

From faith...

to method.

To understand how we arrived at the language so common today, we must now move forward into a different kind of history.

Not the history of doctrine—but the history of method.

And it is there that the modern framework begins to take shape.

Chapter 8

Charles Finney and the Rise of Decision-Based Evangelism

Up to this point, a consistent pattern has emerged.

- Scripture presents salvation as belief and confession
- The apostles preached repentance and faith
- The early church continued without formulas
- The Reformers recovered justification by faith

For centuries, the Gospel remained centered on what Christ had done—and on the call to believe.

But in the 19th century, a shift begins.

Not in doctrine at first—but in method.

And with that shift, the language surrounding salvation begins to change.

A New Approach to Revival

At the center of this development is Charles Finney.

Finney was not merely a preacher.

He was an innovator.

He approached revival not as something to be awaited, but as something that could be produced—if the right means were employed.

In his view, revival was not primarily a sovereign act of God.

It was the result of:

- Proper methods
- Correct presentation
- Immediate response

This marked a significant departure from earlier understanding.

The "New Measures"

Finney introduced what became known as the "new measures."

These included:

- The anxious bench (a designated place for those under conviction)
- Public invitations to come forward
- Direct appeals for immediate decision

These methods were not inherently insincere.

In many cases, they were driven by a genuine desire to see people respond to the Gospel.

But they introduced something new:

A structured moment of response.

From Proclamation to Persuasion

Historically, the pattern had been:

Preach the Gospel → Call for repentance → Trust God with the result

With Finney's approach, the pattern began to shift:

Present the message → Create urgency → Lead to a decision

The difference is subtle—but significant.

The emphasis moved from:

- The message itself

to

- The moment of response

The Rise of the "Decision"

With this shift came a new way of thinking about conversion.

Salvation began to be framed as:

- A decision made at a specific point in time
- A response that could be observed and measured
- An outcome tied to a visible action

This was not entirely foreign—people had always responded to the Gospel.

But now, the response was:

- Expected immediately
- Structured intentionally
- Encouraged publicly

The internal work of faith began to be associated more closely with an external act.

The Role of Human Agency

Underlying this shift was a change in emphasis.

Earlier preaching had stressed:

- The necessity of faith
- The work of God in the heart
- The power of the Gospel itself

Finney placed greater weight on:

- The will of the individual
- The ability to choose in the moment

- The effectiveness of method

This did not eliminate the Gospel—but it reframed how it was applied.

The Beginning of a Pattern

Finney did not introduce the modern "sinner's prayer" as it is known today.

But he established the framework that made it possible:

- A defined moment of response
- A guided path to that response
- An expectation of immediate action

Once those elements were in place, it was only a matter of time before they became more refined—and more standardized.

Why This Matters

At first glance, these developments may seem like natural adaptations.

After all:

- Is it wrong to call for a response?
- Is it wrong to urge people not to delay?
- Is it wrong to create clarity in how someone should respond?

These are fair questions.

And the issue is not urgency.

The apostles themselves spoke with urgency.

The issue is not clarity.

The Gospel should be clear.

The issue is where the emphasis rests.

A Subtle Shift in Focus

When the focus moves from:

- Believing in Christ

to

- Making a decision about Christ

Something begins to change.

The center of gravity shifts.

Salvation can begin to feel like:

- A moment to be completed
- A step to be taken
- A choice to be finalized

Rather than:

- A reality to be believed
- A truth to be received
- A Person to be trusted

The Long-Term Effect

Over time, these methods shaped expectations.

People began to look for:

- A specific moment of conversion
- A visible act that marked that moment
- A memory they could point to

This created a new kind of assurance:

Not, “I believe in Christ,”

but, “I made a decision.”

That distinction may seem small.

It is not.

Laying the Groundwork

Finney did not complete the shift—but he initiated it.

He moved evangelism toward:

- Structured response
- Immediate decision
- Measurable outcomes

And once that direction was set, future movements would build upon it.

They would simplify further.

Standardize further.

Package the response in ways that could be easily repeated and widely distributed.

Which brings us to the next stage.

What Comes Next

If Finney introduced the framework, the 20th century would refine it.

Mass evangelism, printed tracts, and global outreach efforts would take the idea of a guided response and give it a consistent form.

It is here that the language becomes familiar.

It is here that phrases begin to settle into place.

It is here that the "sinner's prayer" emerges—not as an isolated idea, but as the natural next step in a process already underway.

Chapter 9

The Sinner's Prayer and the Language of Invitation

If the 19th century introduced the framework of decision-based evangelism, the 20th century refined it into something far more recognizable.

The shift that began with method now found its expression in language.

Clear. Repeatable. Transferable.

The Gospel, once proclaimed as a call to believe and confess, began to be increasingly presented as an invitation —often accompanied by a specific prayer.

This is where the "sinner's prayer" emerges into prominence.

The Need for Simplicity

As evangelism expanded—through large gatherings,

printed tracts, radio broadcasts, and global missions—there arose a practical need:

How do you guide someone to respond... clearly, quickly, and consistently?

In large settings, it was no longer possible to engage each individual personally.

So the response itself began to be standardized.

Instead of:

“Believe on the Lord Jesus Christ...”

The message often became:

“Pray this prayer.”

The intention was not deception.

It was clarity.

But clarity, when simplified too far, can begin to reshape meaning.

The Role of Mass Evangelism

Evangelists like Billy Graham brought the Gospel to unprecedented numbers of people.

Stadiums filled. Broadcasts expanded reach. Invitations were extended to thousands at a time.

In such environments, a clear response mechanism was necessary.

People were asked to:

- Come forward
- Make a public decision
- Often, repeat a prayer expressing repentance and faith

This was not yet always rigid—but it was becoming structured.

The response was now something that could be:

- Seen
- Counted
- Recorded

And with that, the moment itself took on increasing significance.

The Printed Gospel

Alongside public evangelism came the rise of printed materials.

Organizations such as Campus Crusade for Christ (now Cru) developed widely distributed resources designed to communicate the Gospel simply and effectively.

One of the most influential was the "Four Spiritual Laws."

It presented the Gospel in clear steps—and concluded with a suggested prayer.

For millions of people, this became their first exposure to the idea that salvation could be expressed through a specific set of words.

Again, the intention was not to replace faith.

It was to guide it.

But over time, the distinction began to blur.

The Language of Invitation

As these methods spread, a new kind of language became common:

- "Invite Jesus into your heart"
- "Ask Christ to come into your life"
- "Receive Him by prayer"

These phrases were often drawn, at least loosely, from passages like Book of Revelation 3:20:

> "Behold, I stand at the door, and knock..."

Originally addressed to a church, this verse was reinterpreted as an appeal to individuals—to open the door of their hearts.

The imagery is compelling.

But over time, the metaphor began to function as a method.

When Metaphor Becomes Mechanism

This is where the shift becomes most significant.

A metaphor—intended to illustrate a relationship—became a mechanism—used to define salvation.

Instead of:

Believe in Christ

Confess Him as Lord

The emphasis became:

Invite Him in

Pray this prayer

The language changed.

And with it, the understanding began to change as well.

The Standardization of the Response

By the late 20th century, the "sinner's prayer" had become widely accepted as:

- The way to respond to the Gospel
- The moment of salvation
- The basis for assurance

Children were taught to repeat it.

Adults were guided through it.

Churches adopted it as a standard practice.

It was often presented with sincerity—and received with sincerity.

But something subtle had shifted.

The New Center of Assurance

With the rise of the sinner's prayer, assurance began to anchor itself in a different place.

Instead of:

"I believe on the Lord Jesus Christ..."

It became:

"I prayed the prayer."

This created a new reference point:

A moment in time

A set of words

An experience to remember

And for many, that moment became the foundation of their confidence.

Even if little else changed.

The Problem of Substitution

To be clear, a person can pray—and genuinely believe.

The issue is not that people speak to God.

The issue is when the act of speaking replaces the reality of believing.

When the prayer becomes:

- A substitute for repentance
- A replacement for faith
- A guarantee of salvation

Then the focus has shifted from Christ to the act itself.

And once that happens, it becomes possible for someone to:

- Say the words
- Complete the moment
- And yet never truly believe

Why It Spread So Widely

The success of this approach is not difficult to understand.

It offers:

- Clarity in response
- Simplicity in presentation
- Measurable outcomes
- Immediate assurance

It answers the question:

"What do I do now?"

With something concrete.

And in doing so, it provides a sense of closure.

But the Gospel does not ultimately offer closure in a moment.

It calls for faith in a Person.

A Necessary Distinction

We must be careful here.

The existence of the sinner's prayer does not invalidate the sincerity of those who have prayed.

God is not limited by our vocabulary.

Many have come to genuine faith in Christ in moments where words were spoken, prayers were offered, and hearts were turned.

But sincerity does not define the standard.

Scripture does.

And Scripture consistently points us back to:

- Belief in the heart
- Confession of Christ as Lord

Not as a formula—but as a reality.

Recovering the Language of Scripture

The issue before us is not whether we should eliminate all expressions of prayer in response to the Gospel.

It is whether we have allowed those expressions to replace the language Scripture actually uses.

Because when the language changes, the understanding often follows.

And when the understanding shifts, the foundation of assurance may shift with it.

The Question That Remains

At the center of this discussion is a question that cannot be avoided:

Is a person saved because they prayed a prayer…

or because they believed on the Lord Jesus Christ?

The New Testament answers that question clearly.

And if we are to speak with the same clarity, we must be willing to examine not only what we say—but how we say it.

Chapter 10

Assurance: A Past Moment or a Present Faith?

Up to this point, we have examined the language of salvation:

- What Scripture says
- How the apostles preached
- How the church historically understood it
- How modern phrasing developed

Now we come to where all of this becomes deeply personal.

Assurance.

Not in theory—but in the quiet moments when a person asks:

"Am I truly saved?"

And the answer to that question often reveals where their confidence rests.

Where Do We Look?

When someone seeks assurance, they instinctively look somewhere.

The question is not *if* they look—but *where*.

For many, the answer is immediate:

“I prayed a prayer.”

“I went forward.”

“I made a decision.”

A moment is identified. A memory is recalled.

And that becomes the anchor.

But Scripture directs our attention elsewhere.

The Biblical Anchor

In Romans 10, the foundation is clear:

- Believe in your heart
- Confess with your mouth

The emphasis is not on a past event, but on a present reality.

Not:

“Did you once say something?”

But:

"Do you now believe?"

This distinction is critical.

Because saving faith is not something that exists only in memory.

It exists in the present.

The Nature of Faith

Faith, by its very nature, is active.

It is not merely something that happened.

It is something that continues.

A person who believes:

- Trusts Christ
- Relies on Him
- Looks to Him

Not just once—but continually.

This does not mean perfection.

It does not mean the absence of doubt.

But it does mean that faith is not confined to a single moment in the past.

The Risk of Misplaced Assurance

When assurance is tied primarily to a past event, a subtle danger emerges.

A person may say:

"I know I am saved because I prayed the prayer."

Even if:

- There is no ongoing belief
- There is no evidence of repentance
- There is no desire for Christ

The memory replaces the reality.

And over time, that memory can become untouchable—immune to examination.

But Scripture never points to a past action as the basis for assurance.

It points to faith.

Faith That Endures

The New Testament consistently describes faith as something that endures.

Not because a person is strong—but because the object of their faith is.

True faith continues.

It may struggle.

It may grow slowly.

It may be tested.

But it does not disappear entirely.

Because it is rooted not in human effort—but in Christ Himself.

The Role of Confession

Confession, too, is not a one-time event.

It is the ongoing expression of belief.

A person who truly believes does not outgrow confession.

They continue to acknowledge Christ as Lord:

- In word
- In allegiance
- In identity

Not perfectly—but genuinely.

A Better Question

Instead of asking:

“Did I pray the right prayer?”

Scripture leads us to ask:

“Do I believe on the Lord Jesus Christ?”

This question is both simpler—and more searching.

It cannot be answered by memory alone.

It must be answered in the present.

The Evidence of Direction

While assurance is not based on works, faith does not exist in isolation.

It produces direction.

A person who believes begins to:

- Turn from sin
- Turn toward God
- Desire what is true

Not flawlessly.

Not without struggle.

But with a real shift.

This is not the cause of salvation.

It is the evidence of it.

The Danger of False Confidence

One of the most sobering realities is that a person can have confidence—and be mistaken.

Not because they intended to deceive.

But because they were taught to look in the wrong place.

If someone is told:

“You are saved because you prayed this prayer,”

Then their assurance is tied to something that may not reflect true faith.

And over time, that confidence can remain—even if belief is absent.

The Simplicity We Must Recover

The New Testament does not complicate assurance.

It does not send us searching for a perfect moment.

It directs us to Christ.

- Who He is
- What He has done
- Whether we believe Him

Assurance rests not in:

- What we said
- What we did
- What we remember

But in:

- Whom we trust

A Present Reality

The question of assurance is not ultimately about the past.

It is about the present.

Not:

“Was there a moment?”

But:

“Is there faith?”

Because where there is true belief:

- There is reliance on Christ
- There is confession of His lordship
- There is a turning toward Him

And where those are present—even imperfectly—there is reason for confidence.

Returning to the Right Foundation

This does not mean we discard every memory of when faith began.

Those moments can be meaningful.

But they are not the foundation.

The foundation is Christ.

And the evidence of that foundation is not merely that we once spoke about Him—

but that we now believe Him.

The Question That Matters

In the end, assurance comes down to a single, enduring question:

Not:

"Did I say the right words at the right time?"

But:

"Do I believe on the Lord Jesus Christ?"

That is the question Scripture asks.

And that is the question that must be answered—not once, but continually.

Because true assurance does not rest in a moment we can recall.

It rests in a Savior we trust.

Chapter 11
Recovering the Biblical Gospel

We have traced the language.

- From Scripture
- Through the apostles
- Across church history
- Into modern expression

We have seen where clarity was preserved—and where it began to shift.

Now we come to the necessary question:

How do we return?

Not to a time period.

Not to a method.

But to clarity.

Not Reinventing—Recovering

The goal is not innovation.

The Gospel does not need to be improved, refined, or reimagined.

It needs to be understood—and spoken—as it has already been given.

Recovery means:

- Removing what has been added
- Restoring what has been obscured
- Speaking with the same precision as Scripture

Nothing more. Nothing less.

The Message We Must Keep

At its core, the Gospel remains unchanged:

- Christ died for sin
- Christ was buried
- Christ rose again

He is Lord.

And the call remains the same:

- Repent
- Believe
- Confess

This is the message the apostles preached.

It is sufficient.

It does not require enhancement.

The Response We Must Clarify

If the message is clear, the response must be equally clear.

Not:

"Pray this prayer."

Not:

"Invite Jesus into your heart."

But:

- Believe on the Lord Jesus Christ
- Turn to God
- Confess Him as Lord

This does not eliminate personal expression.

People will speak.

They will pray.

They will call out to God.

But those expressions must flow from faith—not replace it.

Speaking Without Substitution

We must be careful not to substitute helpful language for biblical language.

Illustrations can clarify—but they can also distort if they become the primary framework.

When we say:

“Ask Jesus into your heart,”

We may intend to communicate relationship.

But if that becomes the central message, it can obscure:

- The necessity of belief
- The reality of repentance
- The lordship of Christ

The result is not clarity—but confusion.

Teaching With Precision

Recovering the Gospel requires more than correcting phrases.

It requires teaching with care.

Especially:

- With children
- With new believers
- In moments of urgency

We must resist the urge to oversimplify at the expense of accuracy.

Clarity does not require reduction.

A child can understand:

"I was wrong—and I am turning to God."

"Jesus is Lord—and I believe Him."

That is enough.

Urgency Without Pressure

The Gospel carries its own urgency.

- Sin is real
- Judgment is certain
- Christ is the only Savior

We should not hesitate to call people to respond.

But urgency must not become pressure.

The apostles called for repentance.

They did not manufacture responses.

They trusted the power of the message—and the work of God.

We must do the same.

Removing False Foundations

For some, recovering clarity will mean revisiting what they have trusted.

This is not a call to doubt for its own sake.

It is a call to examine the foundation.

If assurance rests in:

- A prayer
- A moment
- A memory

Then it is worth asking:

Do I believe on the Lord Jesus Christ?

If the answer is yes, then assurance rests where it should.

If the answer is uncertain, then clarity is not something to avoid—it is something to pursue.

Speaking to the Church

This recovery is not only for individuals.

It is for the church.

For:

- Pastors
- Teachers
- Evangelists

- Parents

We must consider how we speak.

Not just what we intend—but what we communicate.

Because over time, language shapes understanding.

And understanding shapes belief.

Returning to Simplicity

The Gospel is not complicated.

It is direct.

It is clear.

It is sufficient.

- Believe in your heart
- Confess with your mouth

Not as a formula—but as a reality.

Not as a method—but as a response.

The Weight of Words

Words matter.

Not because they save—but because they reveal.

They shape how we understand truth.

They frame how we respond.

And when they drift, even slightly, they can lead us away from clarity.

Recovering the biblical Gospel requires that we speak again with the same words—and the same meaning—that Scripture gives us.

The Final Call

In the end, everything returns to the same point.

Not a method.

Not a moment.

A Person.

Jesus Christ.

Crucified.

Risen.

Lord.

And the call remains unchanged:

Believe on Him.

Confess Him.

And rest—not in what you have said—

but in who He is.

Chapter 12

How Should We Present the Gospel Today?

After everything we have examined, a practical question remains:

If we set aside formulas, scripted prayers, and familiar phrases—

how should we present the Gospel?

This is not a theoretical question.

It is the question asked in living rooms, hospital rooms, conversations between friends, and quiet moments when someone says:

"What do I need to do?"

If we are to recover clarity, we must be able to answer that question simply, truthfully, and without confusion.

Start With the Message

Before considering the response, we must be clear about the message itself.

The Gospel is not:

- A self-improvement plan
- A spiritual enhancement
- A way to feel better about life

It is the declaration of what God has done in Christ.

At its core:

- Jesus Christ is the Son of God
- He died for sin
- He was buried
- He rose again
- He is Lord

This must remain central.

Not assumed.

Not implied.

Spoken.

Because faith must have an object.

And that object is Christ.

Speak About Sin Honestly

The Gospel has no meaning apart from sin.

Not as a general idea—but as a personal reality.

People must understand:

- They have sinned
- They are accountable
- They cannot save themselves

This does not require harshness.

But it does require honesty.

Without this, repentance has no context—and belief has no urgency.

Call for a Response

The Gospel is not merely information.

It calls for a response.

That response is not complicated:

- Repent
- Believe
- Confess

These are not steps to complete.

They are the description of what it means to turn to Christ.

So when someone asks:

“What should I do?”

We answer clearly:

“Turn to God and believe on the Lord Jesus Christ.”

Or simply:

“Believe in Him—trust Him.”

Resist the Urge to Script the Moment

There is often a temptation to guide the moment toward a specific outcome.

To make it clear.

To make it complete.

To make it measurable.

And so we may feel the need to say:

“Repeat this after me.”

But Scripture does not model this.

The apostles did not script responses.

They proclaimed Christ—and called for belief.

This requires restraint.

It means allowing space for:

- Thought

- Conviction
- Genuine response

Not silence—but not control.

The Right Place for Prayer

Prayer is not removed from the moment.

But it must be properly placed.

A person who believes will often pray.

They may:

- Call out to God
- Ask for mercy
- Express their trust in Christ

This is natural.

But the prayer is not what saves them.

Faith is.

Prayer is the expression of that faith—not the mechanism of it.

So instead of saying:

"Say these words,"

We can say:

"If you believe, speak to God. Call on Him."

And allow their words to reflect their heart.

Speaking With Children

Children require clarity—but not distortion.

We do not need to replace biblical language to make it understandable.

We can say:

- "You have done wrong—that is sin"
- "Jesus died and rose again"
- "You need to turn to God and believe in Him"

And for repentance:

"I was going my way—now I turn to God."

Children can understand this.

What they need is not simplification that removes meaning—but clarity that preserves it.

One-on-One Conversations

In personal conversations, the approach remains the same—but with attentiveness.

- Listen carefully
- Speak clearly
- Ask questions that reveal understanding

Instead of rushing to a conclusion, we can ask:

- "Do you believe that Jesus is Lord?"
- "Do you trust Him?"
- "Do you understand what it means to turn to God?"

These questions do not replace the Gospel.

They help bring it into focus.

Urgency Without Pressure

There is urgency in the Gospel.

Life is uncertain.

Judgment is real.

We should not hesitate to say:

"You should not delay."

But urgency must not become pressure.

We are not responsible for producing a response.

We are responsible for proclaiming the truth.

God is responsible for the heart.

When Someone Responds

When someone does respond—when they express belief—there is no need to validate it with a formula.

Instead, we can:

- Affirm the truth of the Gospel
- Encourage them in their faith
- Point them toward baptism and obedience

Assurance is not given because they said something.

It is grounded in what they believe.

What We Must Avoid

In recovering clarity, we must be careful to avoid replacing one formula with another.

The goal is not to create a better script.

It is to remove dependence on scripts altogether.

We must avoid:

- Reducing salvation to a moment
- Anchoring assurance in words spoken
- Measuring success by visible responses

These may feel effective.

But they can obscure what matters most.

Trusting the Gospel Itself

At the heart of all of this is a question of trust.

Do we believe that the Gospel itself is sufficient?

That:

- The truth of Christ is enough
- The call to believe is clear
- The Spirit of God is active

If we do, then we can speak simply.

Without embellishment.

Without substitution.

With confidence.

Returning to Simplicity

In the end, presenting the Gospel does not require creativity.

It requires faithfulness.

- Speak the truth about Christ
- Speak the truth about sin
- Call for repentance and belief
- Trust God with the result

That is enough.

It has always been enough.

And when we return to that simplicity, we are not losing something.

We are recovering what was never meant to be replaced.

Chapter 13

A Final Appeal: Believe and Confess

There is a simplicity to the Gospel that we often struggle to accept.

Not because it is unclear—

but because it is so clear.

We have a tendency to add where God has spoken plainly.

To structure what He has left simple.

To define what He has already declared.

And in doing so, we sometimes move the focus—just slightly—away from where it belongs.

This book has not been an argument against sincerity.

Many have come to Christ in moments shaped by familiar phrases, guided prayers, and well-meaning instruction. God is not constrained by our language. He saves in spite of our imprecision, not because of it.

But sincerity is not the standard.

Scripture is.

And Scripture speaks with a clarity that does not require improvement.

What Remains

After everything has been examined—after the history, the language, the methods—what remains is what has always been there:

Jesus Christ.

Crucified.

Risen.

Lord.

And the call remains unchanged:

Repent.

Believe.

Confess.

Not as steps.

Not as a formula.

But as the reality of turning to Him.

The Question That Matters

In the end, the question is not complicated.

It is not:

“Did you pray the right words?”

“Did you have the right moment?”

“Did you follow the right process?”

It is this:

Do you believe on the Lord Jesus Christ?

Do you trust Him—

not in theory, but in truth?

Do you recognize who He is?

Do you rest in what He has done?

Do you confess Him as Lord?

That is the question Scripture asks.

And it is the only one that matters.

Where Assurance Rests

Assurance does not rest in:

- A prayer once spoken
- A moment once experienced
- A decision once made

It rests in Christ.

In who He is.

In what He has accomplished.

And in whether you believe Him.

Not yesterday only.

But today.

A Word to the Reader

If you have relied on a phrase—

on a memory—

on a moment you cannot quite understand—

this is not a call to fear.

It is a call to clarity.

If you believe in Christ, then your assurance rests where it should.

If you are unsure, then do not look backward.

Look to Him.

Not to what you said—

but to who He is.

Nothing More Is Required

The Gospel does not demand that you say the right words.

It calls you to believe.

To turn to God.

To trust in Christ.

To confess Him as Lord.

Nothing more is required.

And nothing less will do.

The Final Word

The New Testament never asks:

"Did you invite Jesus in?"

It asks:

"Do you believe?"

And it answers:

"Whosoever believeth on him shall not be ashamed."

That is enough.

It has always been enough.

Believe.

Confess.

And rest—not in what you have said—

but in the One who has been raised from the dead.

Appendix A: Common Phrases Examined

Language shapes understanding.

Over time, certain phrases have become deeply embedded in how the Gospel is presented. Many of them are used with good intentions. Many have been associated with genuine moments of faith.

But intention does not always preserve clarity.

In this appendix, we will examine several common phrases:

- What people usually mean when they say them
- Where they may introduce confusion
- How we can speak more clearly

The goal is not to criticize—but to refine.

"Ask Jesus into Your Heart"

What Is Meant

This phrase is typically intended to communicate:

- A personal relationship with Christ
- Receiving Him inwardly, not just intellectually
- A desire for Him to dwell within

It aims to make the Gospel feel close, personal, and accessible.

Where It Can Mislead

The phrase is not found in Scripture as a description of salvation.

It can unintentionally suggest that salvation is:

- An act of invitation
- Something initiated by the individual
- Completed by saying the right words

It also introduces ambiguity:

- What does it mean for Jesus to "enter the heart"?
- How does one know if it has happened?

Over time, the metaphor can become a mechanism.

Instead of pointing to faith, it can replace it.

A Clearer Alternative

Rather than saying:

"Ask Jesus into your heart,"

We can say:

- "Believe on the Lord Jesus Christ"
- "Trust in Him"
- "Turn to God and believe the Gospel"

These phrases come directly from Scripture and carry precise meaning.

"Accept Christ"

What Is Meant

This phrase is often used to express:

- Receiving Christ personally
- Not rejecting Him
- Responding positively to the Gospel

It attempts to convey openness and willingness.

Where It Can Mislead

"Accept" can imply:

- A passive acknowledgment

- Agreement without transformation
- A decision without repentance

A person can “accept” something as true without placing their trust in it.

In this way, the phrase may fall short of the depth of biblical faith.

A Clearer Alternative

Instead of:

“Accept Christ,”

We can say:

- “Believe in Him”
- “Trust Him”
- “Follow Him as Lord”

These expressions emphasize reliance, not mere agreement.

“Make a Decision for Christ”

What Is Meant

This phrase highlights:

- The need for a response
- The responsibility of the individual

- The importance of not remaining neutral

It seeks to create urgency and clarity.

Where It Can Mislead

While salvation does involve a response, framing it primarily as a “decision” can shift the emphasis:

- From faith → to choice
- From trust → to action
- From Christ → to the individual

A decision can be made without true belief.

It can also place assurance in the act of deciding, rather than in Christ Himself.

A Clearer Alternative

Instead of:

“Make a decision for Christ,”

We can say:

- “Believe on the Lord Jesus Christ”
- “Turn to God”
- “Trust in Him”

These phrases retain urgency while keeping the focus on faith.

"Give Your Life to Jesus"

What Is Meant

This phrase is often intended to express:

- Surrender
- Commitment
- A willingness to follow Christ

It highlights the cost and seriousness of discipleship.

Where It Can Mislead

While surrender is a real aspect of following Christ, this phrase can suggest:

- That salvation is achieved through commitment
- That a person must first offer something to receive something
- That the emphasis is on what we give, rather than what Christ has done

This can subtly reverse the order of the Gospel.

We do not give in order to be saved.

We believe—and then we follow.

A Clearer Alternative

Instead of:

"Give your life to Jesus,"

We can say:

- "Believe in Him"
- "Trust Him as Lord"
- "Follow Him"

This preserves both faith and the call to discipleship—without confusing the two.

"Pray This Prayer"

What Is Meant

This phrase is used to:

- Guide someone in expressing repentance and faith
- Provide clarity in a moment of response
- Help someone who may not know what to say

It is often offered with care and sincerity.

Where It Can Mislead

This is perhaps the most significant area of concern.

When a person is told:

"Pray this prayer and you will be saved,"

It can lead to the belief that:

- The words themselves secure salvation
- The act of praying is the decisive moment
- Assurance rests in having said the prayer

This can result in:

- False confidence
- Misplaced assurance
- Confusion about the nature of faith

A person may pray without believing.

And yet feel certain because they completed the action.

A Clearer Alternative

Instead of:

"Pray this prayer,"

We can say:

- "If you believe, call on Him"
- "Speak to God—tell Him what you believe"
- "Turn to Him and trust Him"

This allows prayer to remain—but as an expression of faith, not a substitute for it.

Holding Language Carefully

None of these phrases are necessarily used with wrong intent.

Many have been spoken in moments where real faith was present.

But over time, repetition gives language weight.

And when that language becomes the primary way the Gospel is understood, even small imprecisions can grow into larger misunderstandings.

Returning to Biblical Clarity

Scripture gives us language that is:

- Clear
- Sufficient
- Unambiguous
- Believe
- Repent
- Confess

These are not outdated terms.

They are precise terms.

And when we use them, we are not making the Gospel harder to understand.

We are making it clearer.

The Goal

The goal is not to eliminate every familiar phrase.

It is to ensure that whatever we say points clearly to what Scripture says.

Because in the end, the question is not:

“What words did we use?”

But:

“What did we mean—and what did they understand?”

And if we can answer that with clarity, then we are speaking in a way that aligns not only with intention—

but with truth.

Appendix B: The Gospel in Scripture: A Clear Reference

Clarity does not come from creativity.

It comes from returning to what has already been said.

Throughout this book, we have examined the language of salvation as it appears in Scripture. This appendix gathers those references into one place—so that the reader can see, plainly and directly, how the Gospel is presented in the Word of God.

Not summarized by tradition.

Not reframed by method.

But stated as it is written.

The Core Message of the Gospel

The Gospel is not a concept—it is a declaration.

In 1 Corinthians 15:3–4, it is defined succinctly:

> "Christ died for our sins...
>
> He was buried...
>
> He rose again the third day..."

This is the foundation.

Everything else flows from this reality.

The Call to Believe

The most consistent response called for in Scripture is belief.

In John 3:16:

> "That whosoever believeth in him should not perish, but have everlasting life."

In John 3:36:

> "He that believeth on the Son hath everlasting life..."

In Acts 16:31:

> "Believe on the Lord Jesus Christ, and thou shalt be saved..."

Belief is not presented as optional.

It is central.

The Call to Repent

Alongside belief is repentance.

In Mark 1:15:

> "Repent ye, and believe the gospel."

In Acts 3:19:

> "Repent ye therefore, and be converted, that your sins may be blotted out..."

Repentance is not separate from belief.

It is the turning that accompanies it.

The Confession of Christ

Faith does not remain hidden.

It is expressed.

In Romans 10:9–10:

> "If thou shalt confess with thy mouth the Lord Jesus, and shalt believe in thine heart... thou shalt be saved."

Confession is not a ritual.

It is the outward declaration of inward belief.

Calling on the Lord

Those who believe call upon Him.

In Romans 10:13:

> "Whosoever shall call upon the name of the Lord shall be saved."

This is not a formula.

It is the natural expression of faith.

Salvation by Grace Through Faith

Salvation is not earned.

It is given.

In Ephesians 2:8–9:

> "For by grace are ye saved through faith... not of works..."

This establishes the foundation:

- Not by effort
- Not by performance
- Not by ritual

But by grace, through faith.

The Simplicity of the Response

When asked directly what must be done, Scripture answers plainly.

In Acts 16:30–31:

> "What must I do to be saved?"
>
> "Believe on the Lord Jesus Christ..."

No additional instruction is required.

The answer is complete.

A Summary in Scripture's Own Words

If we were to summarize the Gospel using only the language of Scripture, it would be this:

- Christ died for our sins and rose again
- Repent and believe the Gospel
- Believe on the Lord Jesus Christ
- Confess Him as Lord
- Call upon His name

This is the message.

This is the response.

No Formula Required

What is most striking about these passages is not only what they say—but what they do not say.

They do not instruct:

- A specific prayer to repeat
- A phrase to memorize
- A formula to complete

They present truth—and call for faith.

For the Reader

If you are searching for clarity, you do not need new language.

You need these words.

Read them.

Consider them.

And ask yourself:

Do I believe this?

Not:

Have I said something?

But:

Do I believe?

Because the promise of Scripture is not tied to what you have spoken—but to whom you trust.

Final Clarity

The Gospel is not hidden.

It is not complicated.

It is not reserved for those who master a process.

It is declared openly:

Believe on the Lord Jesus Christ, and thou shalt be saved.

That is the message.

And it is enough.

A Final Request

If this book has helped bring clarity to your understanding of the Gospel, I would like to ask you for a small favor.

Would you consider leaving a review?

Reviews do more than provide feedback. They help others discover this message—especially those who may be asking the same questions you have wrestled with:

- What does it truly mean to be saved?
- What is the Gospel—really?
- Where should my assurance rest?

Even a short review—just a few sentences—can make a meaningful difference.

How to Leave a Review

On Amazon, simply scroll to the review section and click:

"Write a customer review"

You might consider sharing:

- What stood out most to you
- What clarified your understanding
- How the book impacted your perspective

Thank You

Thank you for taking the time to read *Believe and Confess: Recovering the Biblical Gospel.*

More importantly, thank you for taking seriously the question at the heart of it:

Not, "What did I say?"

But, "Do I believe?"

— Victor M. Font Jr.

www.ingramcontent.com/pod-product-compliance
Lightning Source LLC
LaVergne TN
LVHW030921080826
845145LV00013B/3006

* 9 7 8 1 6 2 4 2 2 0 6 5 4 *